NEURAL NETWORKS

Neural Networks Tools and Techniques for Beginners

Table of Contents

DISCLAIMER

ABOUT THE AUTHOR

John Slavio is a programmer who is passionate about the reach of the internet and the interaction of the internet with daily devices. He has automated several home devices to make them 'smart' and connect them to high speed internet. His passions involve computer security, iOT, hardware programming and blogging.

What are Artificial Neural Networks?

We use Python Here and Here's Why

Artificial Neural Networks are digitized nodes designed to mimic the biological nodes of the brain to complete computerized tasks. That's about as tiny of a definition for ANN's as you will ever see, but normally when one asks the "what" question, they also ask "how does it work" because that usually provides a better explanation of the "what" question. Therefore, the rest of this book will cover the "how does" for neural networks.

It's Easier to Conceptualize In

The reason why Java and Python are really popular within college environments is due to the fact that they are easier for conceptualizing various computer science topics. The reason why we use Python within this book to explore code examples is due to the fact that it has a relatively simplistic concept that can be expressed through very meaningful syntactical words.

It's the Most Popular Option

Python is also the most popular option for handling any advanced machine learning or computer vision algorithm. This is particularly because Python is a primary language used by science researchers, which means that along with the C language, Python receives special attention from the inventors of these algorithms.

It has the Most Access

As it is the most popular, it will also have the most access when it comes to different algorithms. While algorithms like the A * algorithm is a popular algorithm amongst many languages, subjects like Hough Lines or Hough Contours are rather uncommon in languages like JavaScript. Even though JavaScript is a fantastic language, it isn't one of those languages that are on the forefront for handling computer vision and neural networking. Sure, there is a JavaScript solution for these things and there is a tensor.js that came out not too long ago, but

Python is the one that's going to be capable of handling a lot more functions.

Let's start with Algorithms

A Deceiving Algorithm: The A * Algorithm

$$f(n) = g(n) + h(n)$$

This may look like a foreign concept to you, but if you have played any video game that involves an enemy attempting to follow you, you have encountered this algorithm. Specifically, imagine you have soldiers and they need to get to you as quickly as possible in order to keep you engaged in whatever game you are playing. That's right, this algorithm represents what is known as pathfinding. n is the last node on the path, g(n) is the cost of the path from the start to n, and h(n) is the estimated cost to the end of the path (using the shortest way).

Pathfinding is a really deceiving algorithm that looks like it could be machine learning. The problem is that pathfinding is a Brute Force tactic with some clever recursive algebraic equations that requires the algorithm to know where the end of the algorithm is. Therefore, once your enemy soldier spawns into the room, it begins with two basic variables. You have the variable that contains where the enemy soldier is in the room and you have where you are in the room. Normally, these are considered X & Y coordinates.

What the algorithm does is it finds the shortest path to you but because it is clearly evident when an enemy simply runs to you, developers employ deceiving tactics. You see, essentially, they allow the pathfinding variable to take breaks or get within a certain radius so that the enemy can stop and fire behind a cover of some sort. This makes it seem like an enemy soldier has gotten to your location and is smart enough to take cover.

Then, if you decide to hide for long enough, the developer may also employ the tactic where it waits until a certain amount of time has passed and if you have not shot bullets, the algorithm tells the enemy object to continue on its' pathfinding algorithm. This makes it seem like the computer has adapted to your over defensive demeanor and comes after you.

As I said, this is a very deceiving algorithm that many people have often dubbed as artificial intelligence without realizing that its simple illusionary tactics at play. The reason why I point this out is because machine learning is about prediction; it does not know where it will end up. If you were ever wondering if an algorithm is a machine learning algorithm, you simply have to wonder if the output is not based on an external force separate from the algorithm but from an internal force inside of the algorithm. There are a lot of algorithms out there that provide The Illusion of machine learning when there's not a single bit of machine learning involved.

Understanding Recursive Algorithms

```
ml.py                          ✕

1
2   def recursive(value):
3       if value > 0:
4           print(value)
5           value -= 1
6           recursive(value)
7           pass
8       pass
9
10  recursive(6)
```

```
6
5
4
3
2
1
[Finished in 0.5s]
```

As you can see from the code above, we have a simple recursive

program that simply takes the number, prints the value, subtracts one,

and then calls on itself again. At the heart of machine learning

algorithms, recursive algorithms are how the machines learn. On a very

basic and conceptual scale, you have a machine learning algorithm take

in an input and then that machine goes through several neurons in the

neural network to eventually produce an output. However, if you were to change and altar the different neurons for better predictions, you need to have it not only push the input through to the other side but also push it back through so that it can reconstruct the data. This is important to make sure that the algorithm is working correctly and is not mangling any of the data.

However, whenever we talk about Recursive algorithms, the first one to be mentioned is usually the Fibonacci sequence. This is because the Fibonacci sequence has such an important role in mathematics that it is the common factor when talking about recursive algorithms. You can only get the Fibonacci sequence by using a recursive algorithm. Machine learning is different from the Fibonacci sequence. Machine learning takes the data and adapts given a certain situation.

Understanding Adaptive Recursive Algorithms

```python
1   import random
2   def node(value):
3       if value % 4:
4           bias = random.randrange(1,10,1)
5           print("Node Bias: " + str(bias))
6           return bias
7       else:
8           bias = 3 if value % 3 == 0 else 4
9           print("Node Bias: " + str(bias))
10          return bias
11          pass
12      pass
13  def recursive(value):
14      if value > 0:
15          print("Value: " + str(value))
16          if value % 2 == 0:
17              value += node(value)
18              recursive(value)
19          elif value % 2 == 0 and node(value) >= 6:
20              value -= 2
21              recursive(value)
22          elif value < 1:
23              print("Value completed at: " + str(value))
24              return
25          else:
26              value /= 2
27              recursive(value)
28              pass
29          pass
30      pass
31
32  recursive(10000)
```

```
Value: 10000
Node Bias: 4
Value: 10004
Node Bias: 4
Value: 10008
Node Bias: 3
Value: 10011
Value: 5005.5
Value: 2502.75
Value: 1251.375
Value: 625.6875
Value: 312.84375
Value: 156.421875
Value: 78.2109375
Value: 39.10546875
Value: 19.552734375
Value: 9.7763671875
Value: 4.88818359375
Value: 2.444091796875
Value: 1.2220458984375
Value: 0.61102294921875
Value completed at: 0.61102294921875
[Finished in 0.7s]
```

9

Now, what you see here is a *much more* complex recursive algorithm and that is because it is an **adaptive** algorithm, which means that the algorithm **changes** based on certain conditions. First off, let's clear something up, this code was only meant to display an adaptive algorithm and does not actually achieve anything meaningful.

Where does it change?

I am glad you asked. Firstly, the program only begins if the number is greater than 0 as seen in line 14 and then it ends once it goes below 1 as seen in line 22. This is done to prevent infinite recursion. However; the algorithm becomes something different going from whatever value you put in to the value of below 1.

The change occurred with lines 17 and 19. When we use the node function, we are changing how the recursive function works. As we can see from the output, the node function only affected our value 3 times, but the value went from being an integer to a float by the time it had completed. Not only this, but the algorithm went up before drastically falling. Additionally, with each place value lower, it took significantly more values to reach the next lower place value. Additionally, something particularly odd is that the remaining results after 10011 all end with a 5.

Finally, **what** makes it an **adaptive** algorithm? There is no way for us to predict the outcome of every value put into the algorithm and the definition of the function changes because of certain parameters based on what the next version of the value is in the recursive function. In other words, it adapts to the value provided. While not an exact example, this is how neural networks work as a concept.

Fundamentals of Neural Networks

Understanding the Decision Tree

In order to understand this, we must first assume that you know nothing. Now, knowing nothing, how do you make a grilled cheese sandwich? If you struggle with this parameter, this is essentially the parameter that a neural network has to deal with. Whether you realize it or not, when you make a grilled sandwich you are making a decision tree. This decision tree was first put together by some experimentations and then solidified through practice.

I can remember the first time that I made a grilled cheese sandwich, which erupted in flames because I had the heat too high. Therefore, the next grilled cheese sandwich had the heat at half of the metric that I was using. In this, the sandwich came out alright but eventually, through practice, I found that the best temperature for me to cook these grilled cheese sandwiches was between 60 to 70% of the heat of what my stove could produce.

I know you are probably wondering why I am talking about grilled cheese sandwiches, but I'm talking about what I had to go through and what you have to go through in order to learn how to do a grilled cheese sandwich. When we deal with neural networks, we have to figure out what instructions this machine is going to need in order to produce the result that we want, which requires us to emulate the decision tree we would have.

Let us use the toast part of the grilled cheese sandwich because we would be here all day if we would try to create a decision tree for the entire grilled cheese sandwich.

1. What are the features of "toast"?

Well, it is slightly burnt bread with a little butter spread on one side.

2. How burnt is "slightly burnt"?

3. How much is too "burnt"?

4. How much is too little "burnt"?

5. What is a "little butter"?

6. What is too much "butter"?

7. What is too little "butter?

... There's a lot more that could go here.

As you can see, a decision tree is probably a lot more, but these would likely make you give a syntactical answer. "Too much butter is this... " or "Too burnt is this..." with a likely representation of a picture or a detailed description is what we humans would give, but computers don't understand this... at least, not directly. Instead, we give it a sequence that it remembers and then give each sequence a score. If it is too much, we give it above a 5 or if it is too little then we give it less than a 5.

Alright, let's make a partial "Toast Decision Tree" for our Neural Network so you can see one.

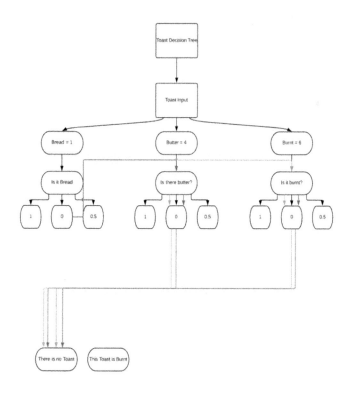

As you can see from the Graph, Decision Trees normally become very massive depending on the complexity of the task. A common tactic machine learning developers utilize is the art of modulating these network responsibilities into their own decision trees. This allows them to tackle the problem without overwhelming themselves when looking at the problem.

Additionally, you'll notice that there's a few that are translated into programming such as No being a 0 instead. This is because that is how it is seen by the program and how it is incorporated. If you've had some experience working with bitwise mapping of pictures, you'll know that this graph is just a tiny sliver of what needs to be done but it does get the concept across.

Without Decision Trees, it's impossible for us to develop any type of learning algorithm. In this case, such an algorithm might be used in a toaster that learns how you like your toast toasted. In the next two sections, we'll talk about weights and biases, which effectively creating the learning aspect of these algorithms.

Understanding Weights and Biases

For a very long time, weights and biases confused me. I understood what they were for but creating them can definitely be a challenge for those new to this. In neural networking, you have something known as a node. A node is a question that accepts an input and has a bias and a weight along with that input.

Not all of these nodes will have a bias and a weight, but they usually do. As you'll see in the picture below this, we have added a node to our decision tree. This node is pretty simple to understand; it is just asking if the toast has got the right amount of butter.

In this instance, I am using the weight to equal 2 as a minimum bar for how much butter is acceptable. The user, the person who normally uses this conceptual Toast machine, tends to have a preference of 6 and we call this a bias. Biases and weights can generally be whatever you want them to be, but they are the minimum and maximum of your neural networking node. Therefore, only when you continuously test this machine against different formations of biases and weights do you get the data you need to train this machine to better recognize how to make toast or, in other words, do what you want.

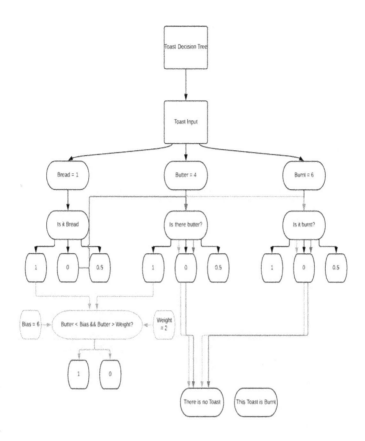

The Three Layers

Input Layer

Everyone comes off as if they understand this layer because it has a very familiar tone to it; "input" is kind of universal in programming. However, this is the Input Layer, not the Input. In the

18

input layer, you're going to have to segment and separate based on the type of information you want to utilize.

In many networking models, you will have to clean, sanitize, and simplify inputs. Let us say that you are going to use images as your input for a Facial Recognition program. First of all, you are not just going to hand the image off as your input directly because you are not going to need all of that information. Instead, you might run an equation like this:

```
0 if (r + g + b) < (255*3)/2 else 1
```

This is a ternary operator that states that if the values for RGB are less than 382.5 collectively, then rgb is assigned 0 but, otherwise, they are assigned a 1. This is a very crude way to create a black and white photograph, but it still represents a very common way to simplify the data.

Once you have simplified the data, you are likely going to have a common 2:3 or a 3:4 matrix that will feed a rather small portion into the inputs for the input layer. This is either done before it enters the neural network or done once the image is received in the neural network depending on the stage you are at with your neural network.

As I have already implied, the input layer not only includes the inputs for the neural network but also includes Data Reduction and Data Compression techniques for faster processing as neural networks already do a lot of processing already before adding any kind of overhead.

Hidden Layer

The hidden layer is where your neural network is basically going to be. The hidden layer is kind of weird because it is referred to as the hidden layer, but most people only talk about this hidden layer when they are asked how their neural network works. Specifically, whenever they talk about the hidden layer they are talking about how that layer works and so when you hear people talking about the feed-forward neural network or the radial basis function neural network, they are really talking about how the hidden layer works.

Output Layer or Output to Input Layer

Rarely do people just accept the output layer as the singular layer where output is going to be displayed. The Output Layer is usually where the next layer of inputs really reside, therefore an Output layer will really wind up being an Output to Input Layer

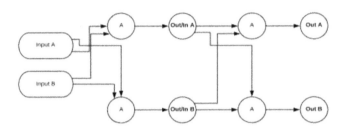

What Neural Networks are Essentially Doing and Why That's Important

They are Computationally Crunching Faster than Humans

It is important to understand that pretty much everything that a neural network can do, a human can usually do. The primary difference between humans and neural networks is the speed at which the task can be completed. Humans have one mind and they can really just do one thing at a time no matter how many people like to say that they can

21

multitask. Scientists have actually proven that you cannot multitask and, if you try, you get worse in each task that you add on to your list.

Because neural networks tend to use processing cores found in the central processing unit or the graphical processing unit, they are capable of doing more than one thing at a time. However, that is also not true because a lot of people think that the central processing unit or graphical processing units are capable of doing more than one thing at a time. In reality, what occurs, is that the processor is switching in between tasks so quickly that it seems like the processor is doing more than one thing at a time when in reality it is just doing one task really fast and then jumps to the next task before the next task can quit and vice versa.

However, even still, because they are capable of relying on such networks, they are able to calculate the mathematics much faster than humans can. Therefore, neural networks aren't really doing anything that impressive, they are just doing it impressively fast.

They are Randomly Predicting with Educational Guesses

It is also important to remember that with neural networks, it's all an educated guess using complex mathematical formulas. Sure, you can train a neural network to guess a little bit better, but the program is essentially using mathematics to get a calculated guess. To be fair, most humans do the same thing and it happens quite often that a human makes a similar guess and is also wrong.

For instance, if you didn't know what a toad looked like and the features of a toad, but you knew what a frog looked like then you could easily look at a toad and guess that it was another type of frog. This is actually a common mistake that happens in children, but you can see where this has been applied because there are very high probability estimates that you have actually committed a similar mistake.

Neural networks work in an educational guess environment and when you train them, all your training them to do is to make their guesses better. Therefore, nothing will be 100% accurate and if it is, it is deceiving you and something is wrong with your inputs, weights, or biases because there is no neural network on the planet that gets to 100% without having a bug in it.

Understanding Network Differences

Neural Networks are not General Purpose

Neural Networks are specifically designed to do one type of job really well and are often incapable of doing more than one job. This has caused the rise of Modular Neural Networks, but this is simply the combination of more than one neural network.

This means that when you develop a neural network, you need to take on the design to handle one aspect per neural network. For nearly a decade, this has been the standard for developing fast and efficient networks. It's important to understand this because many neural networking projects have failed simply because they attempted to create a neural network that did more than one thing.

FNN - Feedforward Neural Network

The current and most simple form of currently in-use Neural Networks is the Feedforward Neural Network because it does not use

Backwards Propagation. A Feedforward Network's most common use is in Image Processing that doesn't require any learning. In these instances, you might use something like the Contourlet method or the Integer wavelet transform and many other methodologies depending on what you are fusing together.

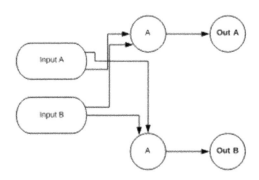

Radial Basis Functions NN

This Neural Network is exceedingly good with interpolation and pixel manipulation. The easiest way to explain the Radial Basis Function NN is with the name itself, which states that everything will be based on a Radius. Basically, it will create several circles where the important data is inside and from then on, it will use that as one of the Radial Functions.

There are several types of Radial Basis Functions such as the commonly used Gaussian (found in Blur effects) or the Thin Plate Spline. Each one is unique and handles the data quite differently. With this idea, a Neural Network then incorporates this function:

$$y(x) = \sum_{i=1}^{N} w_i \phi(\|x - x_i\|)_1$$

Finally, the way that predictions work in this type of network is that the closer the input is to the center of one of the radiuses, the stronger the confidence will be in the prediction.

Kohonen Self Organizing NN

The Kohonen Self Organizing NN way outclasses this book in terms of complexity, but it is important to understand what it does and that it's a glimpse into the lesser discussed algorithms in even intermediate courses.

Primarily, this type of neural networking is actually designed to reduce the amount of neural networking horsepower you might need to tackle a problem. In order for this type of network to be really useful, it has to have an enormous amount of training data. Likewise, unlike most of the neural networks here, this neural network uses a specialized type of learning called competitive learning. While classified as a subset of unsupervised learning, competitive learning is where the nodes of the network versus each other in order to respond to the data. This helps with cluster data.

Recurrent NN

Recurrent neural networks are neural networks that any smartphone user interacts with on a daily basis. Essentially, these types of networks are often referred to as long short-term memory. Therefore, if you said "Good" and it is 6p.m., the same time you said "Good Night" another time before, then the Neural Network will provide an auto selection of "Night" because it is a reoccurring behavior. There are a few different types of memory and recurrent networks depending on what you are trying to achieve.

The Elman network is made up of 3 layers where the middle layer is constantly acting as a context unit. Each "time-step" or the time the network pushes the inputs forward, the network saves the previous hidden layer values via forward propagation. This allows it to continuously apply context to the words at play.

The Jordan network is the far more familiar version of the recurrent neural network as this is the one that constantly feeds the output layer into the neural network instead. These two are classified as the "simple" versions.

Convolutional NN

Convolutional Neural Network is the talk of the town when it comes to machine language and that's because it's kind of like the Hulk but for algorithms. However, like anything that's popular in the computer science world, it's also massively complex so I'll try to break down how it works for you.

Essentially, the primary goal for a CNN is to break down the image (as they are primarily used on images) into smaller, much more notable features. Normally, the images are turned into grayscale and then convolutional mathematics run on that section of the image. This allows the neural network to find minute patterns in features that are not noticeable on the large scale.

As I have said multiple times, neural networks have been with us for a very long time. We are just now gaining the ability to take pictures of checks with our smartphones for depositing them into our banks as of writing this book but LeNet-5 was created in 1998 and could do exactly that. The only problem was that we simply didn't have the hardware in our pockets. The reason why I have stopped providing algorithms is due to the fact that we are talking about neural networks that require their own book because they're so complex.

Modular NN

A Modular Neural Network is really a collage of different neural networks and is considered to be the final step for neural networking. Essentially, what it means is that you combine two or more networks to get multiple tasks done. For instance, you could run a convolutional neural network on an image to see if there are any patterns in the image, but you could also run an object character recognition algorithm as well as a facial detection algorithm to detect the restaurant name in a photo with the name of the person who is standing underneath the sign.

Activation Paradigms

Activation Functions or Paradigms?

Remember that neurons are the primary basis for how neural networks work and that neurons are actually based off of the neural networks inside of our own brain. Therefore, we have to have a way of signaling whether the neuron should go off at all or if it should go off. These are called activation functions because it determines whether the neuron should be activated or not. There are several different activation functions or activation paradigms because there are several different instances in which the variations will be used.

Step or Threshold Function

Threshold functions are by far the most commonly used activation function inside of neural networking because they just make sense. In the most basic terminology, a threshold function simply determines whether the number is above or below a specified amount, which then determines whether something should be fired or not fired. Therefore, it might look a little something like this:

```
def sign(value, x):

    return 1 if ((value * weight) + bias) > x

    else 0

        pass
```

This is a very basic function that returns a 1 or a 0 based on the calculated result of value multiplied by weight plus bias is greater than x.

Linear Function

A linear activation function is a little bit trickier because it is basing it on whether it conforms to a linear equation. Therefore, the equation usually looks like:

$$X = YZ$$

In the programming language, it would look something like this:

```
def linear(value, z):

    return (value * z)

    pass
```

You might actually already be able to tell the problem with this function because it does not help with complexity at all. It really just creates a linear line.

Sigmoid Function

For this next one, be prepared to take an enormous leap in complexity because the equation for the Sigmoid Function is:

$$A = \frac{1}{1 + e^{-x}}$$

I will never understand how one could make such a leap in such complexity, but the Sigmoid function is pretty useful. First of all, it is non-linear, so it can handle XOR problems, which we'll talk about later on. Not only this, but it shows a clear difference in changes when applied on a graph between two points. However, there is a problem

with this type of function because it is not *vanishing gradient* friendly.

In neural networking, you can have many layers in your hidden layer.

However, a gradient is something that travels through all of them.

Therefore, imagine if your network had three nodes and one layer.

Altogether, it's not that bad, primarily because it only has a possibility

of 9 connections for 3 outputs. However, what if you added the layer

with another three nodes? Well, this would then jump up to 18

connections, and then 27 connections, and then 36 connections.

However, it is highly unlikely you are also only going to have just three

nodes, so, what if we have 5. By the time we reach our 5th layer of

connects, we have a total of 125 different connections for our gradient.

It quickly becomes a problem because now the changes in our

algorithm are much less substantial past the first layer.

In the programming language, this sigmoid function would look like:

```
def sigmoid(value):
```

```
    return 1 / float(1 + Math.exp(-value))

    pass
```

Tanh Function

Tanh is the evolution of the sigmoid function and it is literally just a scaled version of the sigmoid, but it comes with a significant advantage. The gradient is much stronger when it comes to tanh and is often much more widely prefered than sigmoid as a result. The equation for this is

$$A = \frac{2}{1 + e^{-2x}} - 1$$

ReLu Function

Finally, we reach the ReLu Function, which is by far the choice for many of the complex networks out there. It is a step algorithm in a sense, but here's the equation for ReLu:

$$A(x) = max(0, x)$$

Now, this can be rather deceptive to newcomers as this equation gives a linear result but ReLu is actually nonlinear. The range for ReLu is also [0, inf], which means this is the compriser of the bunch listed here. You get the benefits of a nonlinear equation with sparse activation, but because the minimum is 0 that means the gradient will eventually reach zero because of complexity. In other words, even though ReLu is awesome, if you make your network too big, it will simply zero out at the end. The solution to this is something like leaky ReLu where each x that is below zero, the y becomes that x multiplied by 0.01. This keeps the neurons firing so that you can recognize issues in the network.

This is Not All of Them And Here's Why

If you can think of a math equation inside of, well, math, then you can probably think of an activation function. An activation function is a yes or no as to whether something should be fired or not. In other words, there are almost as many activation functions as there are mathematical functions in math. Therefore, since I don't really think covering the entirety of math in a single book is truly productive here, I have shown you the most popular of the activation functions used in neural networking.

Learning Paradigms

As of right now, there are three different versions to Learning Paradigms. These are Supervised Learning, Unsupervised Learning, and Hybrid Learning.

Learning Versus Memorizing

One key feature that many machine learning books admittedly tend to leave out is the difference between learning and memorizing because by the time that you get to this level, you tend to just assume the reader will know the difference. It is extremely easy to build a machine that memorizes what is and what is not a specified input. When we talk about machine learning, what occurs is the machine has adjusted weights and biases according to a training set to learn the similarities between the inputs to justify the differences between the inputs.

The key way to find out if your machine is learning or it is memorizing is to run the sample data so that it supposedly learns before submitting completely different data to test if it has learned. If it fails immediately, you will know that something is wrong with your algorithm and it may not even be learning.

Supervised Learning

Supervised learning is the primary way that most neural network engineers will first start making their neural networks. Essentially, it's where you design a neural network, feed your neural network inputs, and check the outputs to see if they worked correctly. You then go in and manually change your weights and biases.

However, there are more complex forms of supervised learning where one example utilizes the ability to randomly select inputs and just bombards your neural network with various inputs to see if any one of them got the right output. You can then use this data to see if your inputs are incorrect or if you need to change your weights and biases.

Needless to say, this is the most common form of developing a neural network and is usually the first step in making a neuron that works, even if you plan to move on to unsupervised learning.

Essentially, neural networks are made in steps and supervised learning is 99% going to be part of that first step.

Eventually, this methodology will give you either Classification outputs otherwise known as Discrete Outputs or Regression outputs otherwise known as Continuous outputs.

Unsupervised Learning

Unsupervised learning is usually the last step in the process if not the secondary stuff. In this learning paradigm, the neural network examines the outputs that it provided to itself and judges whether something needs to be changed inside of the neural network, which it then will change if it needs to. This is usually where self-organizing maps come in to play or some other very clever way of recursively running a neural network where it judges its own success. Here is an algorithm that might help to explain how it does this:

$$f\left(\sum_{i=1}^{n} w_i x_i\right)$$

However, this algorithm might not be enough for you because this is the algorithm for a self-organizing map. Therefore, let us de-abstract a little bit further here and talk about who has long hair and who has short hair. Let us say that we want to determine if an x or unknown is a male or female based on the length of their hair. This X is set to 6 and then let us say that we have an array of

```
men = [1,2,2,5,3,1,1,3,6,7,2,3,3]
```

And then we have another array of

```
women = [1,2,5,8,9,7,7,8,6,5,8,9,6]
```

In these two data sets, we can clearly see a trend and so can our neural network. Our neural network, fed the data, will learn that men generally have a 1-3 length of hair while women have a general length of 5-9, which means that the neural network will guess that X is a woman based on the data with a likely confidence of +60%. This is a very simple thing to figure out, but you might think "it didn't learn anything" because you just calculated for the average. That's right and wrong. If you remember correctly, machine learning is about taking in a previous set of data and guessing correctly based on that data. Since 6 is in both data sets, a memorized algorithm would have just seen six in both but twice in women, so it would naturally go with women but with a 100% confidence. The learning algorithm would see the aggregate data and calculate a confidence score based on how closely 6 correlated with the data set from women. It is unsupervised because we handed it two data sets and then an unknown input, expecting a result without tweaking or testing for anything beforehand.

Hybrid Learning

Hybrid Learning is a combination of Supervised Learning and Unsupervised Learning.

Multilayer Perceptron

What is a Perceptron?

`   Invented in 1957, the Perceptron, itself, made an enormous splash in the technology world for machine learning. The only problem is that the original Perceptron was incapable of learning a XOR function, which is vitally important and a glaring problem. Essentially, it is the neural network that took the inputs and applied a linear classifier to them. For instance, we could even say

```
0 if (r + g + b) < (255*3)/2 else 1
```

Is a Perceptron by itself because it can either be below or above a certain number? However, what if it was *exactly* the divided number? What if it was 382.5, where would I put my output? This is what is known as the XOR problem or an Exclusive Or, it can either be one or the other, but it cannot be both. Luckily, our program languages tend to automatically select one but XOR is still a problem because we cannot leave it up to the programming language to decide.

How does a Perceptron Work?

The Perceptron is often the first ML algorithm taught to those seeking to learn the ways of neural networking as it is the simplest one. This is where you will learn how *most* neural networks handle their information. It all start with this simple equation:

$$wx + b > 0 \rightarrow 1$$

Or

$$X = \sum(w * input) + b$$

Therefore, if the **weight** multiplied by the **input** plus the **bias** is greater than 0 then we want to return a 1. In the second equation, it is the sum of the weight multiplied by the input added to the bias, which will give us our number. Let's begin putting this into a program.

```
testingData = [0]

for x in range(0,100):
```

```
        testingData.append(random.randrange(1,10
,1))

    pass

print(testingData)

def node(value):

    pass

[0, 6, 3, 2, 6, 4, 1, 2, 3, 8, 1, 4, 6, 1, 7,

5, 8, 1, 7, 8, 9, 4, 5, 9, 8, 3, 4, 9, 3, 3,

9, 1, 1, 7, 5, 6, 1, 6, 4, 6, 7, 8, 6, 4, 9,

4, 4, 8, 4, 5, 4, 2, 8, 1, 5, 5, 9, 6, 9, 5,

6, 8, 3, 4, 1, 3, 3, 8, 7, 3, 4, 2, 6, 2, 7,

5, 5, 9, 9, 8, 2, 9, 3, 4, 7, 9, 2, 6, 5, 3,

6, 5, 6, 1, 2, 8, 8, 4, 6, 2, 9]

[Finished in 0.4s]
```

Alright, so what we have here is a randomly generated listed of

numbers for different lengths of hair. I will go ahead and make two versions of this for men and women, with men being a predominate below 5 and women being a predominate above 5.

```python
testingDataMen = [0]

testingDataWomen = [0]

for x in range(0,50):

    if x % 5 == 0:


        testingDataMen.append(random.randrang
e(5,10,1))


        testingDataWomen.append(random.randra
nge(1,5,1))

    else:


        testingDataMen.append(random.randrang
e(1,5,1))
```

```
        testingDataWomen.append(random.randra
nge(5,10,1))
            pass
    pass
print(testingDataMen)
print(testingDataWomen)
def node(value):
    pass
```

```
Testing Data Men = [0, 9, 2, 1, 3, 1, 5,
1, 2, 2, 1, 9, 2, 2, 3, 3, 9, 3, 4, 1, 1,
5, 1, 2, 1, 1, 8, 4, 4, 2, 3, 5, 4, 1, 1,
4, 6, 2, 3, 3, 4, 6, 3, 1, 1, 3, 5, 3, 1,
4, 3]
Testing Data Women = [0, 1, 8, 6, 5, 6, 2,
```

```
    5, 5, 5, 6, 1, 6, 6, 7, 8, 2, 7, 8, 9, 6,

    3, 6, 7, 5, 7, 3, 7, 5, 5, 8, 2, 9, 7, 6,

    8, 1, 6, 6, 8, 7, 3, 6, 8, 6, 8, 4, 6, 8,

    7, 5]
```

As you can see, this gives us a really nice output of 100 different inputs with a clear bias that women will be above 5 and men will be below 5. The input is also randomized so that we can continue to "train" our neural network if we want to take it even further. Now, here is where things get tricky because I am *so tempted* to just write an if statement that just automatically classifies it based on a preset definition, but that is not how a neural network works and it could become **wrong** over time. If women started having shorter hair and men started having longer hair, such an algorithm would need to be manually changed. Therefore, we need to handle a few different things:

1. As of right now, men have short hair and women have long hair, which means the mean of men's hair will be lower than

women's. We need to have the neural network guess which sex is associate with which length of hair.

2. If the guess is wrong, then the number needs to enter the male's or female's "recall" memory.

3. Over time, if male's hair becomes longer and women's shorter, then the mean will naturally change for both sexes.

The first thing we are going to do is create our activation function, which we will be using the "Step" function as we only have 2 possible answers.

Alright, so let's go over how to do the mathematics again. With each input, there is going to be a weight that goes along with it. Therefore, we have something like this occurring:

$$1 \, if \, w_1 x_1 + w_2 x_2 + \cdots + w_n x_n > \theta \, else \, 0$$

Now, if you noticed, the "bias" is not included here and that is because the bias is always considered to be 0 at the start. This is because the **purpose** of the bias is to allow a shift of where the inputs are laid out on a graph *without* changing the graph curvature. Therefore,

49

if we had a linear line, then if we set the bias to 5 then x = 1 would now equal x = 6. It would shift all the numbers to the right by 4 more points in that case. You *do not have to have* a bias.

The **purpose** of adding weights to the inputs is to allow us to create a *linear slope* based on the weights. To find the Y intercept, we have to use $mx + b$ and the only change between that equation and the perceptron equation is that $m = w$.

Alright, so let's clarify my setup here:

```python
testingDataMen = []

testingDataWomen = []

weightsMen = []

weightsWomen = []

for x in range(0,50):

    if x % 5 == 0:
```

```python
        testingDataMen.append(random.randr
ange(5,10,1))

        testingDataWomen.append(random.ran
drange(1,5,1))
    else:

        testingDataMen.append(random.randr
ange(1,5,1))

        testingDataWomen.append(random.ran
drange(5,10,1))
        pass
    # Assigning Randomized Weights
    weightsMen.append(random.randrange
(-1,2,1))
    weightsWomen.append(random.randran
```

```
ge(-1,2,1))
        ♦
    pass

print("Testing Data Men = " +

str(testingDataMen))

print("Testing Data Women = " +

str(testingDataWomen))

print("Weights for Men = " +

str(weightsMen))

print("Weights for Women = " +

str(weightsWomen))
```

What you are seeing here is a few different things. Firstly, I am randomly generating the biased data for both Men and Women, we know that. However, what I am also doing is I am also generating random weights for each of the inputs that I have. This will allow me to get randomized results from my Perceptron. Then we have to set up the code for the Perceptron now that we have the data.

First, we need to setup the Activation function, which I have done here:

```python
def sign(value):
    return 1 if value > 0 else -1
    pass
```

Due to our goal being so simple, I just need to find out if the data is good or bad. We can do this with a very simple Step Function in the form of a Sign Function. Then we need to calculate for the weighted sum, which I do here:

```python
def weightedSum(value, weights):
    sum = 0;
    for i in range(0,len(weights)):
        sum += value[i]*weights[i]
        pass
    return sign(sum)
```

```
pass
```

This allows us to iterate over each of the values in both the data set and the corresponding weights set so that we can calculate the weighted sum. Now, if we look at the way we generate the weights, we will either get a 1 or a -1. This means our value being added will either be the original value or the negative version of that value. Weights will be something we change eventually. Now that we have these two functions setup, it's time to move on to the Perceptron.

```python
def perceptron(men, women, menWeight,
womenWeight):
    resultMen = weightedSum(men,
menWeight)
    resultWomen = weightedSum(women,
womenWeight)
    print(str(resultMen) + " " +
str(resultWomen))
```

```
        pass
```

As of right now, our Perceptron is not really predicting anything

and isn't learning anything. Instead, it's dealing with randomized

numbers. Therefore, now we need to change what we're doing to

change it from a randomized algorithm to a learning algorithm.

However, in order to do this effectively, we need to better visualize the

outputs. This means we're going to be using the most widely used

programming library for Python and that is Matplotlib.

```
        def graphPoints(men, women,
    menWeight, womenWeight):
        b = 0
        men_y = []
```

```python
women_y = []

for j in range(0,len(men)):

    x = men[j]

    w = menWeight[j]

    y = w*x+b

    men_y.append(y)

    pass

for k in range(0,len(women)):

    x = women[k]

    w = womenWeight[k]

    y = w*x+b

    women_y.append(y)

    pass

plt.plot(men,men_y, 'bo')

plt.plot(women,women_y, 'ro')

plt.show()
```

This allows me to at least get a more visual perceptive comparison that is much more preferred over the -1 or 1, but I can already see that there's a problem with this:

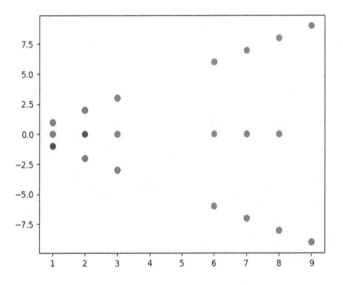

This does, technically, provide me with a visual representation of the data but an inaccurate one at best. While I have found a very clever way of providing the y in this case, I should really have a separated metric for separating men and women. Therefore, I will just

57

use a 1 and a 2 for each x to represent y for male and female. As we can see, this creates a much better result with shorter code.

```python
def graphPoints(men, women, menWeight,
womenWeight):
    men_y = []
    women_y = []
    for j in range(0,len(men)):
        men_y.append(1)
        pass
    for k in range(0,len(women)):
        women_y.append(2)
        pass
    plt.plot(men,men_y, 'bo')
    plt.plot(women,women_y, 'ro')
    plt.show()
    pass
```

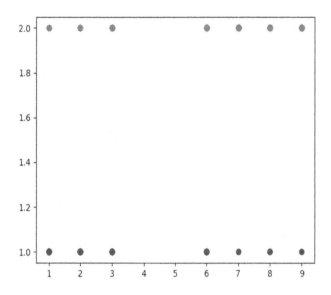

Now it is on to the training, but for training I need to have some solid data, which means I cannot rely on randomized metric anymore. Instead, I am going to take the values for the Testing Data Men and Women and save them as arrays to be used permanently. However, I want to make sure they are -1 as I know this is an incorrect answer.

```
testingDataMen = [6, 1, 3, 3, 3, 8, 2,
1, 3, 2, 9, 3, 1, 2, 1, 9, 3, 3, 2, 2,
```

```
6, 3, 1, 1, 2, 9, 1, 1, 1, 1, 6, 2, 1,

1, 1, 6, 2, 3, 3, 1, 9, 2, 1, 2, 2, 9,

3, 1, 3, 2]

testingDataWomen = [1, 6, 6, 7, 8, 3,

9, 9, 6, 6, 1, 8, 7, 6, 6, 2, 8, 7, 9,

8, 1, 6, 6, 6, 9, 1, 8, 9, 7, 7, 3, 7,

6, 7, 9, 3, 8, 7, 8, 9, 2, 9, 7, 8, 8,

3, 6, 6, 8, 6]
```

This is now the permanent data set I will use to train my algorithm. Now, what I am also going to do is change some of the programming so that instead of running and testing with 1 set of weights, I am going to test against 50 sets of weights. The new code for the Perceptron has changed drastically:

```python
def perceptron(men, women, roundN):
    for m in range(0,len(men)):


        weightsMen.append(random.randra
nge(-1,2,1))


        weightsWomen.append(random.rand
range(-1,2,1))
            pass
    resultMen = weightedSum(men,
weightsMen)
    resultWomen =
weightedSum(women, weightsWomen)
    f =
open("perceptronResults.txt", "a+")
```

```python
        f.write("Round: " + str(roundN)
+ "\n")

        print("Testing Data Men = " +
str(testingDataMen))

        f.write("Testing Data Men = " +
str(testingDataMen) + "\n")

        print("Testing Data Women = " +
str(testingDataWomen))

        f.write("Testing Data Women = "
+ str(testingDataWomen) + "\n")

        print("Weights for Men = " +
str(weightsMen))

        f.write("Weights for Men = " +
str(weightsMen) + "\n")

        print("Weights for Women = " +
str(weightsWomen))

        f.write("Weights for Women = "
```

```
        + str(weightsWomen) + "\n")

        print(str(resultMen) + " " +

str(resultWomen))

        f.write("Men Prediction: " +

str(resultMen) + "\n" + "Women

Prediction" + str(resultWomen))

        f.write("\n--------------------

\n")

        f.close()

        weightsMen.clear()

        weightsWomen.clear()

        pass
```

As you can see, this not only prints to the console now but also
prints to a file that can be cleanly read. Additionally, we now need to
clear the weights and add a slight change to the weightSum function to

handle an IndexError that is caused by *i* no longer being 0 and the

weights just continuously appending.

```python
def weightedSum(value, weights):

    sum = 0;

    i = 0;

    try:

        for i in

range(0,len(weights)):

                sum +=

value[i]*weights[i]

            pass

    except IndexError:

        print(weights)

        pass

    return sign(sum)

    pass
```

This gives a nice big chunk of a data log that I can then build another function for to analyze the results so that I can perfect the prediction table based off of the weights supplied. I can then produce an algorithm that should give me a better weighting score. I would then begin testing it against giant collages of male and female generations to perfect the prediction. Needless to say, we have passed the point where I introduce the concept to you and I begin to spend days of testing the data and making minor tweaks. It is at this point that we have a Perceptron and we are now just making it better. Oh wait, now we have to talk about "Learning Rate" before ending because constantly changing the weights manually is not feasible.

The Learning Rate is determined by the error minus the guess. Therefore, for each weight that was wrong, we set that weight to the error - the guess, which means that if the weight was previously a 1 and the error was 2(the difference between -1 and 1) then that weight becomes -1. Normally, this is an iterative process that takes in one or two inputs at a time instead of fifty, but many have found ways to scale it to that size. This is often known as **Gradient Descent**.

Taking a Dive into Multi-Layer Perceptrons

When we heard that a Perceptron was incapable of calculating for a XOR problem, we took a blunt approach to it: bombard it with a lot more of the same thing… and it worked. This is what we now call a multi-layer perceptron.

Back Propagation

The most popular form of Gradient Descent is Back Propagation, which is a technique that uses the immediate output to calculate where in the network the weights went wrong if it got the label or output wrong. Technically, what we've completed up until this point is known as Forward Propagation.

As I discussed at the end of the Perceptron section, we want to go back over with this technique and this technique is the error - the guess. The goal is to move to the opposite value of the error that we got because it is in the middle where we will find our best result, which is why this is called the Gradient Descent as you are descending the gradient to get to the gradient valley. This is the point where you will need to know Calculus.

How a Multi-Layer Perceptron is Formed

As we mentioned before, the Multilayer Perceptron is designed to handle the XOR problem by throwing more Perceptrons at the problem, but I have not told you what kinds need to be thrown. You see, what we designed is known as an OR perceptron. In other words, the output could be a Female or a Male. There are AND Perceptrons as well that attempt to predict if two things will happen at the same time. These AND Perceptrons can have their values reversed to get Not AND or NAND. With one NAND perceptron, one OR perceptron, and connect the output of those two to one AND perceptron, you can achieve a XOR perceptron.

Practical Application – Text Recognition

Let us be clear here, when I say "Practical Application" I don't mean that I will showing you how to program an Object Character Recognition program as this needs an entirely different book because of complexity. In these 2 chapters, I will explain the concepts behind text recognition and image processing so that you understand how it works.

How It Works

Where are the characters?

Object character recognition really starts with the positioning of the characters. You can have multiple different formats and guidelines that the text follows, which means that there are characters that are read from top to bottom or bottom to top, right to left or left to right. The problem is that when you feed a document into a system, it needs to be able to Chunk Up the difference between the paper and the characters used in the words on the paper.

Therefore, most of the time, the image is turned into black and white and you may think that since the pages are black and white then this qualifies. The problem is that this is not true black and white because there's also different colors. There's the color of whatever you have the paper sitting on, or the lighting on the page that comes from the ceiling, or the reflection of the ink on the page. There's a lot more color in a photograph than you usually realize.

Therefore, the first thing to do for object character recognition is to convert any image into a black and white image. Then we take a few ganders. If the black spots in the photograph are bigger than a certain type of font then we cut those from the image. In this case, it would be useful to section out just the page instead of any background information. From there, we then section out the page from the characters. If you have a page that has one-inch margins, odds are that you are going to want to get rid of those margins since you aren't going to process them. This will only leave the characters left so that they can be segmented and evaluated.

What is the separation of the characters?

The separation of characters is finding out the spaces in a document. You have the manual space bar that you press to separate the words themselves, then you have the space in between the characters, and finally you have the space between the sentences.

In an object character recognition program, the first step is to detect the spaces between the sentences and you do this by comparing the bottoms of all the blacks in one row to the tops of all the blacks in another row. In this case, we would be comparing matrices of zeros.

Once you compared the color to see where the bottom of the characters are and the top of the characters are, you can then separate these characters in two sentences. However, we need to further segment the characters so that they can be processed individually. This is done for speed and to help with neural networking complexity. The next step is to separate the sentences into words. This is done by finding the maximum difference between the right sides of characters and the left sides of other characters. You can then use the maximum difference to essentially crop out the character into singular images.

Once this is done, you can then begin analyzing the characters themselves and this is when machine learning becomes involved.

Features in a Character

Before we bring in machine learning, we first have to figure out how characters will be working for our machine learning. This means that we have to set up specific features that identify the characters inside of our document. Let us look at the letter c. The letter c has a incomplete circle, an arc, in the center but it is different from the letter G because there are no lines going inside of this Arc. There are a lot more things that you can analyze to separate the different characters by their features and this is going to be used as the data inside of the neural networking to compare the original letter to the letter that's being recognized.

Machine Learning Becomes Involved - Like Characters

The reason why machine learning is needed for text recognition is because while you can attempt to use an algorithm to simply analyze the characters, unless those characters are absolutely perfect then you're not going to have a very high success rate. For instance, let's look at the letter c again. If you were to scan in a document and you had the letter c, you might think that your non-machine learning algorithm would be able to pick it up instantly because the letter c should be identical. The problem is no c from other fonts are ever the same. Let us just look at the difference between these two:

C   C

As you can see, we have a Calibri C on the left but an Arial C on the right. While they are very similar, they are not exactly the same. This is why it is vital to compare characters that are like each other rather than exact version, which means that features need to be analyzed by different nodes in a network. This is a very simplified explanation of the complex process involved in recognizing the letters.

Training per Language

Lastly, the point of having a neural network is so that it can break down these different features for other languages. For instance, a Spanish n is different from an English letter n because you have accents put on the letter. For instance, the Spanish word for boy is *Niño* which is definitely different than *boy*. This means that along with character recognition, you also have to have character set recognition in order to provide the right set of characters when recognizing them. Otherwise, a word translated into Spanish from English will only use English letters and English from Spanish will also use English characters.

Where can this be applied?

Text To Speech

There are several applications for this type of software but one of the most prominent ones is translating text into speech for the blind or the mentally ill. Imagine you had a pair of glasses that connected to your phone which allowed you to look at things in your environment that had text, but since you're blind you can't see those texts. Since your phone can take live video and translate the text, it will then read it out to you in a speaker on those glasses. This would effectively allow a blind individual to read something without being able to see and without knowing Braille.

By being able to have glasses on that can read things for you, a person who has recently lost their sight doesn't have to learn Braille immediately. Instead, they can use this as a crutch as they get accustomed into their new life.

Handwritten Notes to Digital Notes

This was a rather popular feature whenever Windows started getting into the tablet world and whenever the company Bamboo came out. Essentially, what the program would allow you to do is it would allow you to either use a sensitive pen to write something on a digital Notepad that took up the screen. By being able to write on the screen, they would then use object character recognition to translate what was written into actual letters.

This was a particularly useful tool for many people taking notes in a lecture and not being able to type fast enough or people who were personal assistants, but it was a rather selective tool. However, this tool is not possible without object character recognition. This is because the program wasn't just allowing you to write notes because that had been possible since we had had the digital sensitizer in screens. The notes would be translated from handwritten into text. This would allow you to do things such as highlighting the text so that it can be changed instead of opening a paint program so that you can erase the words and then insert your own text.

As rarely as this is talked about, object character recognition was and is extremely useful in taking old books and turning them into digital documents. Because older books did not have the Amazon Kindle or the Barnes & Noble Nook, they did not have a digital counterpart. This makes it much more difficult to keep track of, share, and to even find. Instead of going to the search bar on your computer, you would have to go on a search engine and find a library that had it in stock, which you would then go to that library and hope that somebody didn't check it out, and finally you would have to find the book amongst thousands of other books. A non-digitized version of a book is so much more of a pain than a digitized version and it is thanks to object character recognition that we are able to scan them and make these books available via the digital world.

Onsite Translations

This is sort of like the last one but a recent releasing of many apps on the market have revealed on-the-fly translation. Essentially, these allow people to recognize foreign languages and pull up their phones so that they can scan it with their camera without taking a picture and it will automatically translate it. This is really useful for those who are not particularly skilled in a native language to the country they're in and will assist them whenever they maybe tourists but it's also possible that it would be absolutely vital in cases of emergencies should they get lost.

Practical Application – Image Processing

How it Works

Most Times - Convert to Black and White

Image processing works in a very similar manner to object character recognition because, usually, the first step is to convert the image to black-and-white. The reason why the image needs to be converted into black-and-white is because it simplifies how much processing needs to be done. Instead of dealing with a number range from 0 to 255 three times, you simply have to deal with zeros and ones. This makes it vastly more simplistic to deal with, but some prefer different shades of black and white, which still allow for a range of 0 to 255 but still allow for 1/3 the complexity. However, these are usually far more complex algorithms.

Segmentation Matrix

Just as we did with the object character recognition program, image processing is usually segmented into different sections so that features can be extracted from that particular segment rather quickly. These segments are then distributed amongst other neural networks inside of a neural network model. Therefore, if you were to use a facial recognition program then you would want to segment the picture so that the face could be divided into parts. Each of those parts would go to its own neural networking program, which would then decide whether the feature looked like an ear, a nose, a mouth, or some other feature that you chose to have.

This is often referred to as a segmentation matrix because you're taking up the zeros and ones and providing your neural network with a small segment of those numbers in the form of a matrix.

Machine Learning Becomes Involved - Feature or Pattern Recognition

The next step in the program is to actually detect features and patterns, which is done differently based off of the machine learning algorithm that you have. However, if you could imagine a face usually has two ears, one nose, two eyes, a mouth, and, generally, a head, then you understand the concept of features. These would be noticeable features of a face and based off of a certain percentage, you could easily create a facial recognition program that breaks down images into their features to detect faces. However, image processing isn't just about facial features, which is why this section is so open to different algorithms. Image processing is a category of different algorithms.

For instance, you have the artificial intelligence driven automobile control, which is then also separated in-between driver interaction and driver control. In image processing, the driver control would be the artificial intelligence driven automobile control that allows the program to drive the car by itself. In this, there's a camera that is constantly watching each image that comes through a camera via video footage and analyzing what the boundaries are of the road, what features are being seen in other cars, what features are being seen in the pedestrians, and the list truly goes on.

With driver interaction, you might have a program that recognizes the facial features of the person driving the car and maybe measures the mood that the person normally is in whenever they drive. From there, if the person sounds inebriated according to certain parameters then the car could potentially ask for them to prove that they are not drunk. This would require a personality feature recognition program, but these two programs are underneath the category of artificial intelligence automobile control, which is then underneath the wide category of image processing.

Training per Object

Needless to say, because of the wide parameters that could go inside of image processing, each neural networking model type needs through amounts of training. The artificial intelligence driven automobile program has actually been out for a few years but it is still in its testing phases. This is because the neural networking inside of the machine needs to be trained to handle the litany of situations that people are meant to handle.

For instance, if a driver in front of you stops a few feet from where you would normally have stopped in front of a stop light, would you not also slow down your car? Well, the car has to learn that that is something that needs to be done, which is why there is usually a driver that is supposed to keep it an eye on what the program does.

By having a driver in the seat while the neural network is learning, the driver acts as the supervisor in The Learning Experience. The neural network realizes that it was doing something wrong when the driver has to take over, which means that the neural network then uses what the driver does to apply it to future interactions. However, there is so much more to image processing than just AI driving or facial recognition because with image processing, you have the different advantages we have developed for it over the years. This includes heat maps, particle maps, and pretty much anything that has a specialty lens to it. In fact, one of the more notable ventures into image processing is the fact that doctors are now applying machine learning to machines that can diagnose a person without the involvement of a doctor. This would speed up the process of getting patients treated so that Healthcare could be faster, which would then ultimately mean that Healthcare could be made more affordable.

Where can this be applied?

Face Detection

The first and most obvious of these is that image processing can be used in facial detection. However, not only can it be used to identify where faces are but they can also be used to identify who those faces belong to. In fact, we have seen Facebook predict whose face is inside of a photograph based on who uploaded the photograph.

This means that if we were to put the facial detection technology inside of airports, we could feed it a series of highly accurate photographs to allow it to attempt to search for those individuals in the airports. This would allow them to catch any criminals at the airport whether it is international or local based off of technology that's used in pretty much everyday life nowadays.

Object Detection

Most of the time, objects are often detected using several different types of scanners and of those security measures, they are usually ineffective at best. There have been several cases where criminals have still managed to get items on the plane because they found out the weakness of the devices used at these security locations and exploited that weakness. While many of the crimes have been prevented, the fact of the matter is that much of the security is considered to be security theater or something that looks like it is security without being very effective.

If you combined neural networking with things such as a heat map of an entire building, you might get a more effective way of catching these criminals when they think that no one is watching them. The criminal understands that a certain area is a checkpoint, but what they don't understand is that the entire airport is subjected to the same rules.

Using a heat map, you can detect the difference between natural body heat and the objects that people are holding. Comparing that object to a database of objects, one could surmise that a far more effective way of catching these criminals would be employed at these airports without the invasion of privacy. Additionally, there would be no need for the long security lines for the security practices that didn't really work.

Road Detection

This is already being applied in driving practices, but one of the main problems that many countries have is the maintenance of their roads. Deterioration of the road is something that occurs over time and is usually reported by the average individual, but stresses and strains inside of things such as bridges can cause problems if they're not constantly looked after. However, most cities don't have enough money to maintain those bridges on a constant basis without the help of extra taxes or tolls on the citizens that live there.

A neural networking program attached to certain types of sensors placed in those bridges would be able to monitor the bridge without having to have so many eyes on the bridge itself. It would not only be able to generate reports on what's happening to the bridge itself in certain areas, but it would also be able to predict when it needed to be repaired and how much that repair would cost based on what needed to be repaired. Essentially, it would effectively reduce most of the labor force required to maintain such an area of the city.

Additionally, there are also problems that happen within the city that are often designated to private companies. For instance, much of the electricity inside of a city is handled by private corporations. I'm not sure about you, but whenever an outage is reported in a specific area, it takes them a rather long time to fix the problem. The reason behind this is because they have to track down exactly what is the cause of the problem and this means that if an entire neighborhood is without electricity, they have to go to each and every pole to see which poles have electricity and which poles do not have electricity. Then they have to use process of elimination to backtrack from that pole to the original pole that is causing the source of the problem so that they can fix the problem. Finally, they have to diagnose the issue and request for the needed parts if they don't have them. This normally takes hours because not only do they not hire enough people to handle massive situations but the people they do hire are often overloaded with what they already have to do. If the companies employ neural networks and allow the neural networks to monitor the electrical signals coming from the poles, the company would be able to reduce the amount of time needed for process of elimination because the neural network would have kept an eye on these nodes and would be able to tell them which pole was the problem along with a self-diagnosis.

More Accurate Human Motion Detector

Motion detection is really simplistic even though it is often seen as a higher-end technology. What the machine does is it turns the photograph into black and white, with some exceptions using an infrared camera to allow them to detect heat inside of the image. What then happens is that the photo is scanned once to see if there is a change between the previous photograph and the next photograph. If there is a significant change, the motion detector goes off. This is literally Spot the Difference in a computerized form used as security.

A more accurate motion detector is to detect whether there is a human body (or other creature) in the photograph. Remember that the motion detector compares whether there has been a significant difference in the photos in the first place. This means that if you move very slowly across the field of view for the motion detector, the motion detector has a very high chance of not even going off.

However, the human body is generally something that has a head, a torso, and two legs with two arms. If you notice, these are features that specifically describe at least a humanoid object. Instead of detecting for motion, a far more accurate way of detecting whether there is a human within view of the camera is to just use neural networks to see if there is a human featured in that photograph. Then, the camera could track that specific object to see if that object moves at all within the photographs on a pixel by pixel basis so that it has a far more accurate motion detection capture. Additionally, this makes it much faster in terms of processing and allows the camera to take more photographs because it focuses on that featured human instead of an entire photo, which also leads to higher accuracy.

Problems with Neural Networks

They're Sci-Fi

While the general public understand what artificial intelligence is on a general basis, neural networking and machine learning is still something that's usually referred to as something from the terminator. There is a wide majority of individuals that do not want to accept machine learning and neural networks into society. To make it even worse, many people associate various fears with the new technology.

For instance, if a machine can learn how to do something then what job can it not replace? This is a huge and current problem for those on the edge of this technology especially from those who have higher income positions. As of right now, the current solution to such a futuristic problem is to have a global minimum wage. However, this would ultimately be seen as a communist expectation simply because the only ever time that everyone got paid a base rate was in a communist country.

This problem is exasperated by those who do not understand or do not want to take on new and different jobs. You have individuals that have been in the same position for more than one decade and they are usually disgruntled, but okay with having the same job. If machine learning and machines are cheaper at doing that job then a company would be wiser to simply rely on those machines. This would effectively get rid of that particular type of job and so many people associate the new technology of machine learning with global, mass job loss.

This has caused an expectation that those with machine learning knowledge or those who incorporate machine learning knowledge are seeking to get rid of manual labor jobs. While this isn't true, it is currently a stigma in society and often prevents many conversations of progress.

They're New

The next problem is that while the mathematics and concepts for machine learning have been theorized for many generations, the activity of involving oneself with machine learning has been rather recent. It was only in the past decade, once Google and other companies made machine learning services, that a lot of the public in general got involved with machine learning.

While it is great to have such an activity level boost for this specialized field, there's a lot of certification and knowledge statuses that come into play when hiring somebody for this work. Instead of taking an individual inside of their home group, many companies prefer to hire somebody with pre-existing knowledge of machine learning. Normally, these individuals charge a higher rate than the average developer because their knowledge is currently a specialized skill.

Not only this, but these individuals are quite rare. Currently, the technology industry is already having an issue with hiring new developers on a yearly basis. Adding machine learning to the list of skills that one can have to get a job increases the lack of talent pool that currently exists. Even though a lot of companies want to hire a specialist that understands this technology already, many companies have to resort to paying someone in-house to learn how machine learning works and how to implement the technology.

This often leads to common mistakes or months of research that's simply dedicated to advancing the skill of one or many individuals that may or may not leave a company once they have that skill. Due to this risk, many more companies above those that want the machine learning skill often forgo it in order to wait until it is appropriate to hire someone from the market. As of right now, most Hardware companies that have thousands of employees are the only ones capable of teaching a developer in-house without the risk of losing that developer.

This means that machine learning is often a very exclusive talent pool that is hoarded by much bigger companies. Smaller companies, particularly startup companies, simply don't have the resources to dedicate their company to making machine learning part of their process.

Additionally, with the part of this being new comes the part of the lack of Standards. If you look at Ruby on Rails or C++ or Java, these all have standards that developers follow. Due to the fact that the machine learning society is so small right now, there are not a lot of standards for what should be done and how to do it properly. Instead, much of the information is solely centered around what the current machine learning algorithms are and suggestions on where they could be applied. While this is great, this often leads to security issues and a litany of other problems associated with bugs.

You Won't Ever Achieve 100%

Most of machine learning is the art of prediction and because most of machine learning is prediction, you won't ever achieve 100%. Even in the act of using machine learning to find a way to optimize some task, you won't ever achieve 100% there either because there is always more than one way to have a task optimized.

To understand why this might be a problem, let us look at the current problem (that occurred as of writing this book) that Facebook and YouTube currently have. Let us cover YouTube first as YouTube is one of the more notable of the two. As of writing this book, YouTube experienced something called an advertisement apocalypse or adcapolypse, which represented the action of several companies pulling their advertisements from YouTube. This has taken the revenue of several thousand YouTube creators and minimized it to where only the most pronounced creators were able to stay on the platform to have YouTube as their daily job. Fast-forwarding to a couple months later, YouTube is once again under scrutiny because the advertisements, once again, showed up under extremist content. YouTube sets out specific guidelines on what is acceptable for videos on their platform and the only way that creators make money before sponsors and product selling is with YouTube advertising revenue.

In order to combat the extremist content, YouTube uses an algorithm to judge whether the content is of an extremist origin. However, the second scrutiny that YouTube came under was due to the fact that even though their algorithm mostly got all of the extremist content, it was never able to fully get rid of this extremist content.

Facebook, while not as severe, faced a similar issue whenever Mark Zuckerberg went before the United States government to discuss Safety and Security of the users of Facebook. In these hearings, Mark was confronted with a troubling question. Even though Facebook is able to catch most extremist content, the government official wanted to know whether or not Facebook willingly allowed opioid advertisements to remain on Facebook. Facebook heavily relies on learning algorithms to prevent the act of selling drugs and doing illegal content on Facebook. However, because they can never get a learning algorithm that is 100% accurate, they can never guarantee that opioid or some other drug advertisement won't appear on their website.

Scalability is a Per Situation Issue

One of the massive issues that machine learning has right now is the ability to scale for the foreseeable future. Essentially, each problem can be thought of as a factorial problem. Let us discuss this with the Traveling Man Theory. The Traveling Man theory states that between five cities of different distances, one should try to find the fastest route to travel to any of them from each of their locations.

96

This is a tricky mathematical problem that is almost always impossible to figure out and many have failed when trying to do so because the problem is one of a factorial nature. While there may only be five cities, there are 120 different possibilities in which the traveling man can go and because the cities are at different distances to each other, it is almost impossible to easily figure out what the best, most optimized route is.

Now keep in mind here that the Traveling Man only has five variables in the situation and yet it escalated to a prediction level of needing to calculate for 120 different possibilities. In the case of Facebook, if you have 200,000 advertisements being submitted from a single country, how is Facebook going to handle the Traveling Man theory in that situation? How does a machine learning algorithm handle a factorial of 200,000? Well, I could assume that it doesn't handle a factorial of 200,000. In fact, I believe that they have simplified equations so that they don't have to deal with such a massive number.

This means that each time that you need to scale the project for whatever product that your machine learning effects, you have to take into account just how many individuals you are handling. This means that whether you can scale a product or not has to be judged at the creation of that product and then at each stage of the product life during the entire production life. This makes the process of using machine learning extremely difficult and, usually, many companies simply house their machine learning Technologies with bigger companies like Google Cloud and Amazon.

Modularity is Almost Nonexistent

In most of programming, modularity is one of the core principles that people work with on a daily basis. In fact, it is thanks to modularity that some programming parts of a product can be worked on while other programming parts of a product can be untouched while the user uses a product. This allows for minute changes and fixes and doesn't require the entire project to be put on hold. These usually are represented by updates that the developers provide to the public that are then incorporated into previously installed code.

Because of how machine learning works, there is almost no modularity to machine learning code. You have the section where inputs are given to the machine learning code, which are fed through the hidden layer, and finally you either have an output layer or you have a hybrid of an output and input layer that allows you to feed the information back through the system to do something more complex.

This means that whenever you have to make changes to a machine learning algorithm, there are no common steps in place or standards that one should take in order to have part of their code working so that the customers still use it. Instead, the entire code is taken and changed, but then there is a scheduled maintenance where the service is down, and the product can be used so that the developers can incorporate this machine learning algorithm.

This has made quite a noticeable impact and I have a feeling that this impact is shown in Facebook because Facebook frequently requests a user to reload their messenger or service whenever a software update has been made. Therefore, this modularity issue may be something that even Facebook has to deal with.

There's a Lot of Patchwork

There is a ton of patchwork and I can personally relate to this because I have had to create a machine learning algorithm that relied on open computer vision. This task was a two-week-long nightmare because machine learning is written in many different languages but most of the languages built in computer vision are built on the same languages used to access Intel and AMD processor libraries. This means that you only have a few languages capable of Performing open computer vision and so you have to create bridges in between the language that you want to use as a machine learning language and the open computer vision programming library.

This means that there is a ton of Patchwork that can go wrong because building a bridge is basically making it so that the inputs that you use in your primary language are understood by the inputs used in your open computer vision library. There are many bridges to many of the software libraries out there, but because this is such a small section of what it means to be in programming, there aren't a lot of software libraries specifically designed to handle this.

This problem is further compounded by the fact that most of the people who build these Bridges build them for the specific case that they have to deal with. The programmers at this level are capable of writing these bridges without the assistance of others, but people who are new to creating their own open computer vision software are not going to be able to write these bridges. Therefore, you have a very extreme learning curve when it comes to adapting average programming practices to this small niche of the programming world.

Processing is Still Not Fully Optimized

Since this is such a niche part of the programming world, the programs are often very specialized towards the processor that is using them. Unlike things such as gaming engines where there are entire teams dedicated to optimizing functions on specific processors, this industry doesn't receive that type of attention because most of them just optimized for the processor they're using. This means that the general public tends to have issues relating towards optimization for many of the programs because there isn't a lot to begin with.

The reason why this is important is because neural networking is often a feature inside of websites. For instance, if we look at Facebook, the facial recognition is done on the server side whenever the user uploads the video or image to Facebook. This means that Facebook had to specifically optimize their code to work on that server because otherwise their code would be using significantly more processing power. This means that they wouldn't be able to accept photographs as fast, it means the computers would have to work harder, and, generally, it would cost more simply because it wasn't optimized.

For Facebook, this is an absorbable cost at the very beginning but for smaller companies, such as optimization needs to be pre-baked into it otherwise they are going to suffer from exorbitant processing and RAM costs. This is due to the fact that neural networking requires a lot of system cores in order to work effectively.

Conclusion

Neural Networks have a Wide Usability

From text recognition to emotion prediction to simply predicting the numbers of the stock market, neural networks a very wide usability. There are a lot of problems that come with being such a diverse tool, especially for those learning how to use this tool and which parts of the tool can be used for what they want to use it for.

Not only that, there's a lot of ethical problems around neural networks right now considering where they can be used. For instance, when Apple informed the public that the accuracy of their facial recognition program was based off a collection of over 1 billion faces, the obvious question of where they got those faces came up. This has long been a battle about what technology can be used without giving up privacy, which facial recognition is one of these areas where it's questionably gray.

If you add on the risk of letting someone else control the car instead of a human or you add on a human no longer telling you what's going on in the news because machines have rewritten articles automatically, you get into the deeper philosophy of what it means to be human. If machines are capable of doing all of the tasks that humans naturally do to sustain their society, what exactly does Being Human mean?

While machine learning has many uses and neural networks are just beginning their steps in society, there are a lot of ethical questions about where they should be applied and how they should be applied. If we are not careful with how we use neural networks, neural networks may actually be the reason why entire societies fall because they can replace most of the jobs needed on the market.

Neural Networks only work with Complexity and Predictions

However, there is a caveat to the neural networking market. Neural networks are only designed to handle complexity, which means that until we produce a neural network that can break down complexity into simplicity then humans will always be at the forefront of neural networks. Essentially, we will be the thing that allows neural networks to understand what it needs to do to reach that complexity. Even so, much like humans are inaccurate most of the time, these machines will also be somewhat inaccurate even though it's not as much as humans.

It is vitally important to remember that neural networks are specifically designed to make predictions and are in no way perfect. You could spend years and decades training neural networks but because of how neural networks work, you will never get a 100% accuracy. There is no 100% accuracy in life itself because even some chemical reactions that we expect to happen one way 100% of the time have wound up performing a different way at some very rare occurrence. Therefore, there is no possible way to have a 100% accurate machine, but we can have a mostly accurate machine.

Neural Networks have Many Problems

Most of the problems that occur around neural networks isn't really mathematics and that's because we've had the mathematics for these networks for over a couple of decades now. Most of the problems center themselves around philosophy and ethics because of where you can apply neural networks. However, a lot of people might think that the ethics and philosophy are higher scaled than what I'm talking about here. As I mentioned before, you do have the higher philosophy of what it means to be human, but this is not what I'm talking about.

Google created an algorithm that allowed you to look up the things that you related to the most, but the problem with this algorithm is that women had a natural tendency to look up the police background of native Africans a lot more than native Caucasians. Eventually, this wound up as a situation that unfairly target African Americans when it came to issues of law enforcement. Therefore, when looking up African Americans, advertisements suggesting they also take a gander at that person's police record also came up. This naturally created a very small uproar as many people called the algorithm racist, which is impossible to do because programming simply can't be racist, it is only the programmer that has the ability to choose to be racist. If anything, it was the women performing that search that had a collective racial bias.

This is something that is inherently wrong with many of the algorithms because no matter how well generalized we programmers may make something, it is ultimately the user who defines what that something becomes.

Therefore, questions of freedom of speech, safety and security, transparency, and many others that are directly relative to our daily lives come from the philosophy that we need to ask about neural networks. If we have a neural network designed to predict the emotions of people, would such a machine be capable of predicting terrorists before they become terrorists? Would we then enter a state of affairs where it was about predicting criminals more than about catching criminals that have already committed the act? There are a lot of high-level philosophy issues but there are a lot of localized philosophy issues that directly impact our daily lives when it concerns neural networks. For instance, should we take away the rights of driving on City roads if the neural networks have more of a success chance by ensuring there are no humans driving, only computerized drivers? It makes sense to do something like that but then it also removes the freedom of being able to drive the car. There are a lot of problems around neural networks right now and many developers honestly choose to just ignore them so that they can progress through or simply don't even think about them half the time, but they do exist and they are brought up in court systems.

The First Computer Took Up the Size of a Room

I always like to leave off books with a happy note and I know that this conclusion has been rather somewhat downtrodden in terms of what this book is about. However, it is important to remember that the first computer took up the size of a large room and had virtually no laws attached to it. Over time, computers have gotten smaller and technology has generally been an industry where we govern ourselves. When we govern ourselves as developers, we tend to follow logical outcomes and ways of doing things that please our customers. Therefore, most of the time, most of the practices are based on pleasing the developers or pleasing the customers and so almost everyone wins in these cases. However, in order to stay in such an equilibrium, we have to recognize the issues that we have to take on going forward. The issues that I listed here are some of the same issues that we had when we first started messing around with computers and then started messing around with the internet. The internet as well as machines have invaded almost every corner of our lives and they have revolutionized how quickly we obtain knowledge and how we perform our lives. While neural networking is a New Concept in the life of the consumer, we as programmers are the ones changing people's lives for the better, so it is up to us to figure out how to handle these issues so that we can all benefit.